Weavings

Poems
by
Mary Ellen Branan

BLUE LIGHT PRESS ❖ 1ST WORLD PUBLISHING

1ˢᵗ WORLD
PUBLISHING

SAN FRANCISCO ❖ FAIRFIELD ❖ DELHI

WEAVINGS

WINNER OF THE 2010 BLUE LIGHT BOOK AWARD

1ST WORLD PUBLISHING
809 South 2nd Street
Fairfield, Iowa 52556
www.1stworldpublishing.com

BLUE LIGHT PRESS
1563 45th Avenue
San Francisco, California 94122

COVER AND BOOK DESIGN
Melanie Gendron
www.melaniegendron.com

COVER WEAVING
by Mary Ellen Branan

AUTHOR PHOTO
Jane Hunt,
Bastrop, Texas

FIRST EDITION

LCCN: 2010939826

ISBN: 9781421891866

WEAVINGS

Acknowledgments:

The following poems in Weavings were published previously:

"Woman in a Circle" in *Gulf Coast Literary Magazine*, Spring-Summer, 1988;

"Shadowing" in *Lyrical Iowa*, Iowa Poetry Association, 1992;

"The Lamp" (as "Exclude the Mark"), in *i.e. Magazine*, Spring, 1993;

"The Shoes at Majdanek," "The Krakow Express," and "The Warsaw Express," in *View points: A Cross-cultural Journal of the Humanities*, Torun, Poland, 1996;

"Reluctance of the Broom" and "Selah Ranch, Texas" in *The Texas Observer* in 2004;

"Drought: Bastrop, Texas" (as Daybreak in a Time of Drought,") in the *Texas Poetry Calendar*: 2006, and reprinted in the anthology *Big Land, Big Sky, Big Hair*, Dos Gatos Press, Austin, 2008.

"Sparrows" in the *Texas Poetry Calendar*: 2009, Dos Gatos Press.

"Circus Bear" in *Reflections*, 60th Anniversary Anthology, Austin Poetry Society, 2009.

"Straw Hat" in the *Texas Poetry Calendar*: 2010.

"Weeds" in the *Texas Poetry Calendar*: 2011.

Notes:
"Woman in a Circle" alludes to an experience in G.I. Gurdjieff's autobiographical *Meetings with Remarkable Men*, E.P. Dutton, New York, 1974.

The concept and some imagery in "Shadowing" is borrowed from Clarissa Pinkola Estes's, *Women Who Run With the Wolves*, Ballantine Books, New York, 1992.

A line in "Weavings" is from Adam Zagajewski's, *Another Beauty*, Farrar, Straus, and Giroux, 2000.

Dedication

I dedicate this book to all those who in the midst of their serial careers always felt there was something more suitable for them; and to those who, looking back, feel they wandered in their quest from their true calling and never found it, or haven't found it yet. And for those who may have found their passion young but admitted later the success and possibility of it waned as youth waned. They can join the late-bloomers, waiting and looking again, exploring, facing forward.

CONTENTS

I

II

III

I

Stonehenge Unvisited

Stones looming against bald sky on British plains,
loaves of bread standing on end,
baking in the sun for five thousand years—
I lost my chance with you.

Not-going to Stonehenge was easy.
A few miles out I loaded my bike on a lorry
and rode up front with the driver,
"too weak," I wrote in my Trip Book,
to pedal round by Salisbury Plain
right up to the Henge.
I could have leaned my bike on a Portal Stone
and stretched like Tess did on a fallen Sarsen,
sinking to its hard mystery.
Now one circles the Henge at a distance,
near the highway, parking lot, and gift shop.

Trip Book says I climbed out at Stockbridge,
cycled the last nine miles to Winchester
and "cooled my heels" at the "finest youth hostel in England."
I laughed at Louise when she pedaled in.

I could yet see Cumberland, Avebury, Orkney, or Clava.
feel electro-magnetic fields on my skin,
have my engine die near Dartmoor Moat,
and see the stones move at Cornwall.

On Mid-summer's Eve, I could climb on a boat
and disembark at Far Hebrides.
I'd meet the Families-Who-Belong-to-the-Stones,
join the crowds winding the double way.
I'd call out with everyone in the Old Language—
they'd teach me the words—*O Shining One*—!
I'd feel the palpable Presence come sweeping along.

Working in Yellowstone: 1959

By midnight the whole summer crew
stuffed the napkin-holders,
leveled off salts and peppers.
readied two giant coffee urns
for the flick of the switch at day-break.

By midnight, we were miles away
and off the highway,
sunk to our chins in a hot, chalky pool,
faces soft in years and the mist,
legs thrust into icy water below,
just where the sulfurous flow from the Springs
meets the Yellowstone's dash to Montana.

Drowsy, we climbed the bank in the dark
and groped for the bundles of our clothes
and found them by the glimmer of pearl-gray Stetsons
on stacks of jeans and identical sweatshirts
we all wore to set us apart from the dudes.

One night, as we nonchalantly lay
facing north toward Gardiner—
half in hell-water,
half in ice-melt,
basking at once in a muttering hot
someday cataclysmic volcano*
and the chilling daily Cold War—
we saw the sky in melting ribbons
move sideways, ripple, and flash like opals.

*The "Yellowstone Earthquake," 7.5 on the Richter scale," occurred August, 17, 1959.
There were 28 fatalities in adjacent E. Idaho.

What Older Brothers Are For

From the foyer she watched him
lunge his head and torso through the bedroom door,
catch the molding with the side of his foot,
and push off for the nearest chair.
He'd somersault down the arm to the cushion,
hitch up to the other arm, and then, swinging,
grasp drawer-pulls with his toes,
and hurling arms over the top of the bureau,
hang on for a moment, panting.
Like that, he'd take the bedroom by surprise
over the floor of glowing lava.

Or lean from the kitchen into the living room.
She admired his lift off, his folding over the radio,
swinging to hook a knee on the davenport.
bouncing sideways along three cushions,
an easy time that whole side of the room.
But near the corner window sill, heel-and-toe,
a clumsy trip-up launched him, laughing, turning in air,
white ash when he touched the floor.

School days, when he was away,
she'd stand at a corner of the living room,
square herself, stare at the floor,
and tall and stately, float on air across the room—
smoothly, silently—inches above the floor!

Years she practiced the Walk
till one day, in a burst of trust,
maybe bragging a little, she told him.
He, of course, must see for himself,
so she stepped into commonplace.

For Children Only

We'd crawl no little distance to a hole we knew
and could barely put our heads and shoulders through.
We'd stand and clamber up into
the belly of the house.

The lower half of the stairs angled there.
The straight wall was the back of the closet.
We had our flashlights, also candles,
muddy knees and skinny cricket bodies.

We had the difficult journey to the pitch dark
of a secret, inviolate place.
The phone sat beyond the inverted steps.
We were in a separate Other space.

We didn't burn down the house.
The phone through the stairs never rang.
No one sat talking, unsuspecting, mere inches away
and said anything we shouldn't hear.

Sometimes, someone trudged up the steps
or hunted for something in the closet,
hangers jangling, so close and unsuspecting.
They couldn't get at us, the children,
walled, roofed, smelling of wood and earth.

Riding the Greyhound

When I used to ride the Greyhound north on
Louisiana 165,
we came to the towns: Oberlin, Glenmora,
Oakdale, or Kinder, seven or eight at night.

I'd put aside the novel I was reading
and look out—hand cupped against
my own reflection—at street-lamps bleeding
through the woods, at lives I glimpsed

in neighborhoods nearing the towns.
Even in early dark, I knew all that mattered
in white frame houses or trailer grounds,
housewife hands over the dish rattle,

fry of onions in the pre-fab's
kitchen, springeri on the porch
of a "brand-new modren brick-on-slab"
a block or so from Glory Hill Church.

Once at a red light, a woman in a pick-up
stuck out her tongue at me, well, because—!
The Hound pulled out in a cloud of dust,
and I had the dark for my nausea.

Making a Movie

Nancy, when she lived in Kingston, Jamaica,
circled an ad in the *Daily Gleaner*
and appeared on the appointed day
with her youngest, Teddy, only four.
She confessed some present need to pretend
in a grownup way, to merge with a crowd
of Europeans, whites
playing themselves in panic,
to run with them along a steaming train,
like wildebeests in full stampede,
mid shouts of gangway! and the dictatorial,
red-faced, pretend-conductors, reaching
for lifted luggage from the steps of battered cars.

In West Indian sun she sweated, with Teddy by the arm,
as he looked back at the camera on its dolly,
little family fleeing the Congo.

Fiercely weeping anonymous Nancy wonders
Why are the husbands staying behind?
Her character would've packed a basket for the train,
a few most precious things,
and wept goodbye on the neck of the cook,
not dreaming of the timbers piled down the track
or mayhem rising, Mau-mau swarming up the bank—.
Nancy hurries, pretending, obeying
the ones who had a grasp of the whole,
how her part fit in.

Woman at the Window

A woman appears at my window,
mere yards between us,
but my living room's dark to her;
She doesn't look, thinks no one's here.

Unconcerned, she bends at my faucet,
drinks, splashes her face.
I stand from the desk and move closer
to bare feet, bare legs, a day-glo pink nylon jacket.
She takes a long time with the water,

then sits on the lawn, jacket thrown beside her.
A lacy edge droops beneath the muddy shorts;
the camisole for bed or underwear stretches across her ribs.
No plan, running on a mild winter day.

She stands a long moment, then paces,
holding a page of newspaper to her chest,
now squarely facing me, me inside unseen.
Some teeth are gone, face thin and rough.

No plan. I could step into light at the window.
Or open the door? In the dark I wait.

A neighbor's car nears, she gathers herself,
strides down the sidewalk with a purposeful air,
bare feet and spectral legs,
having turned the jacket inside-out
and draped it over her head,
hiding in all that light.

SINGLE GIRLS' DREAMS

For Martha

In Kurosawa's *Dreams*, the mother comes out
when it starts to rain to get the laundry,
holding an umbrella over her head, and then
banishes her young son from the house
because he looked at the foxes who carried umbrellas
and passed by in the lane.
Watching the foxes is a definite, if inexplicable, error,
and the boy must leave at once
to search for the foxes,
and beg their forgiveness.

We were twenty-something, stretched out
in hammocks strung between palms at Pie de la Cuesta—
to watch how the vast Pacific drowns the sun.
We wanted adventure
when each day seemed a blue yawn.
A waiter brought us coconuts with gin,
and beyond our toes, the palms, and the steep surf,
the sun did sink like a dollop of hot papaya.

We rose at last and found an eager driver
to rush back to Acapulco, where
with every twilight, fatalistic young men
dive off the cliffs to the chop eighty feet below,
and diners pause for a moment, forks mid-air.
Your fawning admirer sprang from his chair
to chase the photographer who'd taken a picture
of him and you, and tore out the film.
He mumbled some excuse to you, as a boy might
who'd opened an umbrella in the house.

We had a few laughs, cigarets, and cocktails.
That was a paper umbrella
you were holding against the rain.
You laughed a lot,
unlike foxes or angry mothers,
to smooth things away, saving illusions
of romance in balmy evenings, a Rich Man.

Now the sun sinks into the Iowa prairie,
(where I live now),
while Gandarva-ved, the most ancient music,
plays on the Sony, slowly rising to a whirl
of a thousand umbrellas in a vortex,
bringing on the hours as they should be—
such music—if we could play it loud and long enough.

Window Framed

The leafless wood is a darker smudge
beyond a row of triangles of dredged gravel
like ransacked pyramids of Giza,
all brumbled brownish-gray,
a dust of snow on casual ridges.

Behind the farthest pyramid,
the mast of a sailboat on a trailer
draped with rotting canvas
cuts a strong diagonal.
A rectangle shed on the same parking lot

hides the stern of the boat.
The woods against the overcast sky,
fray at the top, a filigree
which could dismember a kite
merely to demonstrate territory.

Gray trunks devour light
and also birds alive, should one enter
among the muted stripes,
spindly trunks,
the perpendicular.

To Have and Have Not

A boyfriend she'd left behind,
a guy who was yet attractive,
who smelled of engine oil and Old Spice, and,
occasionally, cigars,

a guy she could spy on if she wanted to
at work in an arcane engine-oriented place
next door to where she worked herself—
resigned and went his way.

Two weeks too late, she stopped by,
asked,"Where's Jack? Tell him I'm out here."
Her left heel spiked an iridescence on the concrete.
"Jack? He doesn't work here anymore."

Jack? Free-to-leave-Jack?
She hadn't even guessed.

Reluctance of the Broom

A week or two slides by.
One day I notice my tracks in the hallway dust.
Finally, on a Sunday morning
when I can see things more clearly,
but still reluctant, I reach in the twilight
of the pantry wall for the broom.
I probe squarely into corners as if I mean it,
annoyed all along at the straws
the broom itself adds to the crumbs
and the way the fluffs of cat-hair float off
in the turbulence and my own gymnastics
of repeat and repeat,
bent double over the dustpan,
wishing, despite the logic of consequences,
that things would remain in stasis,
that lint, wall-paint, spider legs, my epidermal
layers, that all bones and ashes,
or the events in one single day,
all that fine detritus of disintegration—
would cease transforming
into something to be swept away.

THE LAMP

Li Po, I call the old man who stands on water
in the scene on my Chinese lamp.
Li Po tilts his head, looks up beyond the trees
at a white silk sky and three-way sun.
Lester, our friend in Mercy Hospital now,
declares his "spell" means only good for his life.
The artist who painted this lamp
excluded a mark dividing water
from land; there's a craggy islet behind Li Po
to his left meaning water, but a smear
of grass slopes near him to his right.
He has wrinkles painted on his forehead
and a thin, philosophical beard.
Like Lester, at seventy-two, going to college,
and studying art. "But I don't want to be an artist,"
he says, "I just want to know how they do it."

Li Po's walking staff's tucked under an arm.
Up the shore, a tall house nestled under a cliff;
across the lake, near the top of the jar,
mere arches of blue say "mountains."
On the other side of the jar another man,
certain of water vs. land, sits fishing with a pole.
This fisherman never will rise, step out
from his boat, and walk away on the water.

Waking In Squaw Valley

At a summer daybreak in the Sierra Nevadas
I was jolted out of a dream
by my sister's voice, saying, "Mama?",
turning it up at the end so it's a question:
I startled awake to a Jenny Lind bed
upstairs in "the girls' room."

We'd divided the weeks into three shifts
so we could care for her at home, we said,
but it was also a time for learning
the layers of acceptance—our own more than hers.

Dreamers can dream in layers,
protecting sleep, fooling the dreamer.
To escape that time, that place, I undreamed it
and woke myself up truly
to summer mountain daylight.

I dreamed once that I got out of bed
to shut the window across the room
because it had begun to rain.
But, dreaming still, I re-woke myself,
got up again to make everything safe.
Wait! the window's here, not there.
So once more stirred and had to fling myself
out to my actual face, wet with the rain
misting through the screen.

Talking weeks later, we three discovered how
without any clock's alarm
we each had wakened every two hours,
and in the dark taken the thirteen stairs we knew
so well, to turn her in her bed,
as they had told us to,
hoping we were doing the best we could.
14

FACING UP

We sit in a row of Louis chairs
facing the width of the coffin.
My brother opens a folder:
Navy Orders, 1942.

We name six brothers, three sisters,
note his seeming ease in repose,
how his handsomeness and high cheek bones
make us think of the Cherokee ancestral story,
the Trail of Tears from Georgia.

I lift my hand to touch my cheek.
Nancy, touching her face,
admits she sees a family look
she didn't see before.
Iverson, lifting his hand, says
noses and chins start growing again,
taking on an elder resemblance
he has owned too for a while.

We're quiet together, weak and plastic,
our unspoken mutual theory discarded:
that we were somehow self-determined
and mutants, freely ourselves.

Calmly now, we carry our given face,
which others view more than we do,
each day becoming more itself.

THE GHOST

On All-Hallow's Eve, Melinda lifts the what-not from the wall
and swaths it in newsprint, the same for its miniature village,
cottages, church, donkey, and spotted cows.
Around her a billow of dust glitters in sunlight
striking through the window. After all, the village
stood twenty-eight years in its own bit of earth.

The sun's angle through the dust recalls those afternoons
in closet, trunk, and drawer, emptying Papa's room,
our holding up something good and calling, "Who wants this?"
The oaks in the park cast long shadows
on the field where we had played, piled hay for forts,
picked violets and rain-lilies.

Now we toss hangers and shoe-trees, stack clip-boards,
cartons of yellowed paper, warranties on long-dead
appliances, a Masonic book that improbably instructs,
"In event of death, return to the nearest lodge."
We shake our heads over carbons of orders for ship parts,
how he kept out-of-date and useless things.
A letter from a Chinese seaman returning a loan of ten dollars
and a page of trigonometry scored 100 per cent.
We admire that. But toss it in the pile.

We do keep "Children's Letters," mostly v-mail:
my own scrawl, I hope you don't get killed in the war.
But toss, toss: dog's bark for a frisbee in the park.

Then here's a letter from Grandma, dated 1926—
she finally writes to my father weeks after
four of the family had driven night and day for El Paso,
to find Willie in feverish hallucinations,

in fact, in "dieing condition."
Uncle Ed drove away alone in the Buick, leaving
Aunt Pauline and Grandma to take
Willie on the train for Muskogee—too late.
"The men put us off in Pecos, Texas" she wrote.
"The conductor wired on ahead to the undertaker
and hotel and the people generally at Pecos
were real nice to us. There was nothing
you could have done," she said,
"Your brother Willie is gone."

We went on sorting—
who will sort our keepsakes some day?—
while Uncle Willie, a frail, young ghost
fluttered in motes at the window.

Louisiana Dogwoods

Across a still-life landscape
in pale April sunlight
the dusty cars and pick-ups
together wind the gravel road.

I've been a summer fair-weather niece,
never here this time of year
to see the leafless brambles,
mayhaw, huckleberry, all brown.

The young pulpwood pines
still hold to the clay,
trying again on the grades scraped clean by loggers.
The old-growth I saw years ago—
cypress, hickory, beech, and cedar—
don't come back so well and are lost.

In summer we traveled this road,
shoving each other for the front seat
for the long ride to Clarks for a 50-pound block of ice.
We stopped in Kelly for gas
and Orange Crush, RC, or Delaware Punch.

Now as we drive the gravel miles,
I see again and again
a white translucence
glimmering from the undergrowth's tangle,
and the reason slowly dawns on me:
a beauty she saw every spring of her life:
clouds of single dogwoods
lighting the old winter's murk.

New Year's Morning

I open the window to the New Year,
to the doves' ku-ROO and the cardinal's here-here,
to warm air after rain,
I, asunder and floating a little,
as one does after hard dreaming.

My parents in the dream, alive and smiling,
had an air of majesty about them, moving about
in a grand, sprawling house I've dreamed them in before,
this time, more complete than the attic steeps and hallways,
but still, as before, in a state of general remodeling.
When I step out to the wide veranda, Shadow
rises and shakes in her former way to follow.

I looked out at the point of a lake,
flooded now from drenching rains.
A swamped canoe bumped
the half-drowned posts of the dock.
In the brightening distance open water shines.
I thought I could sail and sail through a summer here,
and forsake my small house, my precarious dominion
the solitary, tenuous projects I'm busy with.

I leaned on the railing and watched
the brightening haze dance on the horizon,
till the dream faded to squares of windowpane.
I'm tired hours later, as though I've fought a battle.

Rare August

The ceiling fan, stilled for three chill mornings,
reveals a furry dust along each blade.
The Cicadas too are silent.

I huddle over fast-cold oatmeal,
remembering winter school-day mornings
when there was ice in the ditches
and hard frost flowers on the window to blow at
but never such an August.

From the open window I see dear old Tiger
stagger off the concrete to lie in warmer grass.
Neighborhood noises come in like ghosts
who'd waited at windows till now
for a way into tight houses,
blown back by air-conditioner winds.
Our houses last week baked in an oven,
walls and roofs shrinking a little more each day.

A baby's cry. A canine yap.
Beneath the hood of his car, a neighbor with a wrench.
Clink.

I'm alone in a boat off Ecuador—
pulling oars—hat wrapped in wafting scarves.
I can see everything from everywhere,
down on me, bird's eye, or up at me
through water—whales' eyes meeting my eyes—
the boat rising with the mist
off emerald swells broken here and there
by black smiling heads, great eyes turning
and the spray of whales breathing,
I among them, cool in their breath.

Straw Hat

Two Japanese businessmen waved a camera into your hands
then posed along the granite wall, straight on, unsmiling,
with the San Jacinto Monument in the background
so the snap would say TEXAS, TEXAS
to everyone back in Osaka.

March, wasn't it, windy and bright?
You and I had hats and sunglasses.
My hat blew off and rolled across the pavement.
That night I dreamed my Guatemalan hat blew off,
and I ran after it again, hat lifting and rolling just out of reach,
like a yellow straw of eternal now.

We were the only ones about at the Channel's edge,
where we bought an ice cream,
where the Battleship Texas should have been—
it was away for repairs.
We stared down on the muddy rectangle gouge,
and on our left, a ship from Japan glided through the Channel.

Zoo Bison

Mornings he crops the grass, flicks
and flicks his tail to stir the flies;
noons, waits, the sun on his back,
holding that handsome profile

for the nickel. A shaggy sandstone boulder,
or a triangle rug hung out to air beside a pail
of water, an altitude of massive shoulder,
hypotenuse down to the goatish tail.

Afternoons, reclining, he chews a second time
and a third some switchgrass or smooth mountain brome
or bluestem in summer prime,
growing hump-high where they used to roam.

He masticates, grinds out the cellulose
in sideoats grama, bluestem, the year's seasons—
in needlegrass, switchgrass, and winter oats
and rye—unmindful of the reasons

for public gaze, for his own patient chewing
of grass, for having such a beard,
for rocking side-to-side, unconstruing
the DNA for wild times in the herd.

Audubon Print

Strange to learn
a famous Audubon print,
the pair of Golden Eyes,
I've prized on my wall,

which formerly calmed me—
its diagonal composition of two ducks
against horizonless storm-gray sky,
stopped in mid-air motion—

is painfully, deeply more,
and I was blind. More than beauty
and the craft of an artist's hand,
a realm beyond I did not see.

I so long overlooked the tiny wound
on the fore wing,
missed the apprehension
of doom in his eyes.

For him, falling towards the lower corner,
the shock of mortal injury;
and for her, recoiling at right angle—
in a reflex of escape—

beaks agape,
her webbed feet treading air,
his treading helplessly
the verge of plummet.

DROUGHT: BASTROP, TEXAS

A transient slight freshness
washes the backyard and the deck.
Always summer and humid.
The homeless cat I've fed for weeks
starts up in terror when I show up
and slinks away through the fence.
Has not rained, will not rain,
fires banned in the county.
These morning clouds will burn away
to a hot blue eye.

Will it rain again?
Will the cat forgive my humanness?
Will I succeed with the bougainvillea,
letting it thirst to the point of death
to force it to bloom?
Surely a sort of thought and motive
in the plant—how else to term it?
It *thinks* of death
and the last chance it has for blooming.

The Road Back

How alien the road back from the road I came in on.
At the end of the driveway, I pause uneasily
because no landmark arises left or right
that could instruct which way for the way back—
the perpendicular road lies the same either way I look.

If I turned coming in to the left, I think, then
I turn to the right, going out. But I don't recall
this huge field scattered with white cows grazing
the kingly white bull watching beneath an oak.
How could I have missed all this?

And at the end of the field, a burly fence-turned-hedgerow,
overgrown with whatever sprouted from where birds shat
in a momentary pause years back: cankered hackberry,
prickly ash, thorny rattail, dewberries, kudzu.
And next, a striding Colossus electric tower a hundred feet tall,
new to me! Though I had the same eyes before.

Next a blue double-wide appears, yard strewn with plastic toys,
red, yellow, and a tractor abandoned mid-row in its plowing,
all having jumped the road coming in from left to right going back.
Houses and tractors, rows of mailboxes.
This ninety-degree curve I believe I did make,
coming in, but there could be ninety-degree curves
here and there, going both ways.
And the sun, four hours ago was high overhead,
not like this one, turning gold and larger, above the trees.

How alien the road back, not what I thought I knew,
but I'm seeing more than I did going in.
Now in the distance at last a familiar pace of traffic,
going and coming, the farm-to-market.
Relieved but chastened, I'm wary of altered patterns
and reversals of vision—as a bird on its vast migration
sometimes takes a mirror-image of his true magnetic path,
and flies southwesterly instead of southeasterly.

LEAVING

Marilyn comes over in the middle
of her day pushing sales
to see me off, brings Pepsi's
to cool us in the empty house
after the final flourish
on the carpet and lifting
the Hoover itself to the back of the truck.
Shadow, who accepts in pure trust
all changes save fireworks, sniffs
at Marilyn's clothes
and visibly wonders why
Eastwood hasn't come.
Marilyn hugs Shadow.

She has brought me a basket for the road:
mints, granola bars, yellow pears, and chocolates.
She strolls the empty rooms and sighs.
She stands in the street as we drive off,
hired driver and I,
and I see beyond her
Shadow, no longer my shadow,
watching through the wrought-iron gate.
Shadow thinks I'll be back.

II

Birding Near Głębokie, Poland*

Yellow face and rusty brown stripes
swept back on his crown like rows of August corn,
the Yellowhammer scallops the roadside wires
perch to perch so we'll never catch up.
But I've named him and claimed him,
the first Yellowhammer ever born.

Now he's grown used to us and descends
to walk along the shoulder, "big and long-tailed,"
when, according to the *Guide to European Birds*,
he should be in blackthorn or feeding in stubbled fields.
Cautioned by the field guide, I don't mistake him
for the Cirl Bunting, who's smaller and lacks
the bright rust rump. Perfect Yellowhammer.

I came for the spring air
and a string of ponds we'd read about,
but this empty road's a bad translation of the brochure,
I think we got off the bus too soon,
the weather can't make up its mind.

Still, archetypal Yellowhammer, I found you—
you found me in a deep, elusive place,
while I got lost in a sunlit mist of rain.

* Głębokie, Polish, means "deep."

THE SHOES AT MAJDANEK*

In the gloom we know after some moments
what's here. At first we resist the absurd,
every shoe so second-hand and faithful
to the foot which claimed it first,
shaped to it, as water by the walls of a jug.

Shoes are public, yet personal, even embarrassing,
strewn about a room or lost in the back of a closet.
But here, counted and kept,
one million six hundred thousand shoes.
We step into our well of space, and they

flood the side rooms, cresting at corners,
swelling hip-deep. Wire bins contain them,
receding in triple rows, dimmer and dimmer
away from the light, till our eyes lose them.
Buckles and eyelets, tongues rigid now,

warped soles, and vamps, cut to last
for good and all. Here, white summer pumps—
fashionable—we say—not much change—
small Mary-janes, large brown brogues, awash.
Outside still it drizzles. We hoist our umbrellas.

*At Majdanek, near Lublin, Poland, was a Nazi concentration camp.

Warsaw Express

The checkered suit, florid face, and bloody eyes
of the businessman who found his assigned seat
across from mine and beside the window
was mirrored exactly in our mutual pane.
Thus, his reflected body and face,
with its thin monkish locks
combed forward to disguise the balding,
contended with everything I preferred
to see beyond him: dark forests and fields,
small town shops, and poles with lights.
He muttered drunkenly a word now and then,
the name of a town we weren't stopping at—
he knew the route.

So mostly I had to shut my eyes,
not wanting to catch his, real or mirrored.
His bursts of language in deep bass
waited at me. He would smirk
towards the others in our compartment
when I had nothing to reply, and
somehow turned it at my expense.
Again, he was proffering the Polish Gazette
he'd found on the window-tray,
convinced it must be mine
and I ought to read it.
Which I finally did, studying intently
the titles of American movies playing in Warsaw.

KRAKOW EXPRESS

Women in the fields fill their arms with wheat
they tie with a single stalk and lean five or six shocks
together in a huddle like children in a schoolyard.
And ten feet over another huddle, docile children,
rows of shocks.
No tractors or combines here.
I see gloves, bonnets, sun-burnt arms.
More than a funnel for hot July wind,
our window's a movie of yellow wheat fields,
a screen for a thousand stills running, woman after
woman as the train races, as if the same women,
same stacking and tying, moving in tiny graduated
changes, frame by frame.
For the women our train in middle distance
quickly disappears.
No one waves.

We wish we could ride a slow train,
there could be such a train,
not the usual *osobowy's* wrenching and grinding
from one-minute stands near every holt and hamlet.
Make it a train that starts out once and serenely,
slowly gliding by village, town, and field,
quietly by back door cottage gardens, asters and lettuce,
by storks in the roof-thatch, home from Africa.

We'd have no haste to arrive.
We'd ride through a larger Poland which used to be—
through time the way we used to know it
as children on a train, waving at the women,
and the women in the fields waving back

* The osobowy is a rural "peoples' train," making frequent stops.

In Łazienki Park, Warsaw

A rose garden and long benches
make an amphitheater of roses.

At the pool's margin, a bronze of Chopin,
handsome, restive, larger than life,
surmounts a granite boulder.
A robe drapes the figure's left side
down to the vamp of his narrow boot.

The robe from the left shoulder like an epaulet
rises and twists barley-fashion, gradually becomes
above Chopin's leonine head
the shape of a massive tree, its angled trunk
down to the roots frames his body.

The hands are beautiful.

At two o-clock summer Sundays,
someone in white tie and tails walks
the pool's edge to the paving below the statue
and lifts a white canvas, folds it aside.

Every summer Sunday afternoon
someone plays the piano below the statue
the Minute Waltz, Polonaise, mazurka, etude, preludes. . . .

Listeners in the garden begin to dream
Paris, Majorca and Valdemosa.*
And the roses turn and bloom.

*villa where Chopin and George Sand last lived

Mallards: Czartorysky Park

Puławy, Poland

The chestnut leaves are hands,
fingers curling from open palms,
large and pale like hands,
floating softly aside in the mild disturbance
of our passing feet, drifting back in our wake,
as we waft the way of least effort
zigzag down the hill
to the pond below
to see the mallards.

Many leaves we scatter,
stacked and clumped hands
under our feet, numberless leaves,
we say, and we speak of leavings numberless
yet to come in the cycles of years.

But autumnal thoughts inspire doubt,
and doubt will vibrate out from here
to beyond, and beget our own finitude.
That's the power of doubts,
that's how they work.

The leaves will cartwheel on their fingertips
their while before transforming under snow.
But Polish children gather them now for vases at home,
for color and scent and gaiety.

We reach the pond. Every mallard sleeps,
all violet and mottled browns, along a fallen willow,
bright bills tucked under wings,
but one among them keeps one eye open.

September: Puławy

Up a steep slope from the main street,
the Polish version of the Roman Rotunda
lifts its yellow dome against a pale, blue sky.

I'm astride a stone wall to one side,
rotunda-side foot on the ground, the other foot free
in empty air above some terraced apple trees

that spill steeply down to backyard gardens,
lettuce and asters, to metal-roofed cottages.
The lilting voice of the priest booms for a mile,

as if for a crowd outdoors, from speakers
mounted in Corinthian leaves above the heads
of three old men sitting a bench on the portico—

no spilling crowd for five o'clock mass,
but the weather's fine, and here a taste for them
of independence from too many old women

in scarves, murmuring responses.
The amplified sibilance muffles the traffic below,
along with birdsong and sough of bending grass.

Unmoved by the language, an unremarked stranger,
I will a butterfly two terrace-steps down to turn
and rise towards me. It comes to arm's length

before it flutters back. I command again.
It turns and comes. Retreats. I repeat five times,
and five times more it retreats and returns,

so close the yellow flame warms me,
I reach out my hand, leaning—I could fall,
ripe-apple-scream unheard, hard to the ground—.

I right myself, swing feet to the cobble, and
breasting the waves of priestly timbre, hurry off,
a nymph or the goddess herself running before me.

November First Night

For Margaret

The sky over avenue trees darkened and receded
as we saw in the distance the glow
that made the cemetery an amber wedge
sloping up to the blackness of the forest.
The air perceptibly warmed as we trudged through the snow,
joined the hurrying late-comers.
Snow crunch gave way to wet trudge,
then to ordinary scuffles on dry concrete.
So many boots on All Souls' Eve
defeated the Polish winter.

Odors came in as we neared the light:
hot wax and pine, bruised spruce and juniper:
garlands for sale at shops along the low wall.
Inside the gates, the crowd broke off
into families threading a maze of stone and hedge,
each to a well-known destination.

We watched them hang the garlands
and light more candles, one at every corner,
every grave, more atop the monuments.
In the warmth we unbuttoned our coats,
pulled off mufflers and mittens, envying,
as we basked in the atmosphere,
the folks brushing clean ancestral plots, draping greenery,
embracing neighbors, a kiss on each cheek.

The living will go home through the snow to supper.
The candles will burn all night, gilding
the black forest, sky, winter, and death.

A Bee Institute in Poland

Along the sidewalk home from the bee-store,
I see over the snow-crowned wall straight through the woods,
almost to the bank of the long frozen pond.
The Czartorysky woods are an ink sketch,
snow-laced below with scalloping briars.

My plastic bag swells with honey-comb candles,
salve for chapped skin,
honey from the month of buckwheat
honey from the month of lime trees,
from bee-bodies, bee-work—or not-work, but bee-ing.

Last spring, I watched the hives behind the institute,
bees circling. The gate where I leaned
mumbled with bees, the little store sign
frothed with exoskeletons from a riot, sacrifice, solidarity.
The professors in the hallway were intense and cheery,
giving their lives to bee genetics, bee-lines, and bee-dances.
The clerk at the bee store was cheery too.
She'll go home at two along this walk,
planning what she needs from the shops for *obiad,*
husband home at three from his shift at the fertilizer plant.

Most bees survive the European winter;
workers fly out on clear days,
eat a lot, sleep only a little at night.
Arthropologists in winter write monographs on bees,
and acolytes lean to study,
having chosen their work.

I'm reminded I missed my calling,
never chose a field I could master,
ran from the call, or it didn't call—
merely stared at me with wild golden eyes.
Back in my concrete-block apartment, I'll burn candles,
care for my hands, sit over sweetened tea.

CIRCUS BEAR

Puławy, Poland

Bear's benign face and my own smiling one
beam toward the camera, almost
cheek to cheek, his three times as large.
Mutual trust is obvious.
I've thrown one arm across his chest.

A Saturday, a traveling big-top
served my need for adventure,
why I paid an extra 50 *zloty*
for a snap-shot of me and the bear.

Protesters at the gate
with pamphlets I could just translate—
deplored cruelty to the animals.
I laugh now and say I was checking
if you were content and cared for.

Forgive me, Bear. If not as joyful as I was,
at least don't mind that moment
and this souvenir.
I shall say my Inner Bear
dared to be close and love you.

Yet in the photo of my small daring,
I'm plainly frivolous, and you
dignified, grandmotherly—
as if, instead, it were you loved me.

III

WOMAN IN A CIRCLE

From an incident in Gurdjieff, *Meetings with Remarkable Men*

From a certain Transcaucasian village,
you trod every Wednesday with sandaled feet
the path of your mother's mother and her mother,
down the swelling foothills
to the River Kurd, carrying as always
on market day, your bright new weaving,
chatting with the others, keeping an eye
on Farida's girl who pulls two goats along.

One Wednesday in the season of Ramadan—
more strangers on the road, more rubles
in their pockets to give for fine wool—
nearing the bazaar, while you've stopped
to raise the jug of water to your mouth,
a blur of black and white moves to your left,
then around to the right, and behind you—
remember the shouts and muffled laughter.

And while you lower the jug and wipe your mouth
with the satin back of your hand, you know
the man in the suit crouching now on his heels
with a stick in his hand has drawn a circle
around you in the dust. Sink to your knees.

See Farida's daughter with a circle around her
start to cry and run bang against the air;
her hands question along the invisible wall,
while Armenian schoolboys giggle
and chase the goats. Since you must,
you will sit all day in the circle until
someone with mercy or bored with cruelty
wipes away with his toe a doorway in the dust.

Shadowing

Homage to C. P. Estes, *Women Who Run with the Wolves*

Wild woman has shadowed you for years.
You know because you catch a glimpse,
though, like smoke, she disappears.

She's in your mother's confiding voice
when she didn't know you could hear her;
in certain dreams, old tales, moonrise,
the gleam of the room just dusted,
and in the other contrary face
staring through yours in your wholesome mirror.
Doesn't the pelt rise when you're cornered?

She wants to see who you are,
to see if you're ready to join her in the forest.
Like a wolf she follows to the side,
then crosses the front of the path:
shadowing. From behind a tree,
she peeks half-face
with one golden eye.

Look one day at the shadow you cast and see
no upright woman on two legs, but the lovely shape
of something wild and free.

MARTHA STEWART LIVING

How to choose the best glove for working in the garden;
how to save a sick aralia;
how to discern quality and age in a chair;
how to dye an outspoken K-mart rose-strewn cloth
in a vat of brewed Earl Grey or even Orange Pekoe
to reveal a medieval dream of damask roses;
how to double-glaze a domed bonbon;
to think of a menu of vegetable linguine
with fava beans
and spraying with Pam the measuring cup
so the Karo or honey will pour away clean;
or dipping one's knife in ice-water
while slicing a sticky dough;
to understand for the first time
how the strips of chocolate dough
placed in rows alternating with vanilla
slices to those sudden small checkerboards,
the cookie of the week.

These, the arts of civilization, the decencies of peace,
the beauty of houses and of self-reliance,
the joy in demystifying these hitherto-exotic delights.
Now serve them on a jadite footed cake-stand
and take them to the woods for a picnic,
transforming an ordinary day to a wonder.
On an ordinary day, a day we've all forgotten,
we for the first time let go the chair leg
and stepped alone,
learning how to move in the world,
and the world promised more and more.

Warrior Princess

In high laced boots Zena bestrides the earth
and meets straight-on with her own limpid blue
the eyes of gods. She's dressed in studded leather,
all straps and epaulets, arm bands and cuffs,
and a tunic from below her breasts to leggings
at her thighs, each ample breast swelling up
into silver rounds of arabesque rosettes,
dark hair in bangs and long, tumbling locks

which never interfere with boisterous battle,
when she sings out in joyous soprano and back flips
head over heels, her long sword riding aslant
her back, the knobbed hilt high as her jaw.

My soul knows Zena:
She often saves small villages.
All men respect her; most are in love with her.
Always a small pale woman rides beside her,
writing down her every word and deed.
Zena and Pale Woman do it all for Destiny.

WEEDS

A day between rains I spend weeding,
one hand bare, the other in a red knit glove.
I pluck and pluck, crawling down the lawn.
The forenoon passes.
I fill buckets to the brim with weeds of a dozen sorts.
I am assiduous, slicing to the very root
a henbane—that can't be good—
but a single far-flung *lupinus texensis* I coddle and let be.

I perceive their urgency to emerge, jam down roots,
for trees to flow sap again after long stasis.
To the bone I too am a subject of the Sun.
But I've slept through a season or two,
ambivalent about roots, which pin one down,
and emerging slowly.

While I make hay and witness the willow
reach to sweep the ground,
the fruitless pear tree interpose a leaf,
I decide what is weed, what is not,
and, despite the profligate drift of seeds,
commit myself to a ceaseless pursuit.
I've never escaped ambition.

Landscape Photographer

I survive on bread and beauty together,
butter my hard roll with slopes falling south,
salt a tomato with hay bales and weather.
I hold a while the names of roads in my mouth
to taste them: Lower Red Rock, Camino Real,
Lonesome Dove, and—my favorite—Gotier Trace.
Hungry, I am fed. Creatures large and small
give room at my approach; if human, always
he lifts a palm from the steering wheel, as I do,
too, for him. I rove the great Out-of-doors,
camera in tow, maybe to say goodbye to
this, the present, ephemeral table before me,
as if I artfully might delay the doom
of a beautiful planet that's daily consumed.

Ways of Surviving

I felt someone looking at me.
I looked up to see a smiling face and eyes,
one red-gloved hand lifted to wave
from the rear window of a neighbor's pick-up truck.
I knew her: the full-color, three-quarter face of Marilyn Monroe.
These days she waves at whoever catches her eye
from cars, semis, SUVs, on freeways and parking lots.
I smiled back at her and lifted my hand.

I keep on the table here a polished fist of amber
with a centipede inside, who
one cloudless morning climbed a Baltic pine,
one delicate foot in front of the next,
a moving fringe wafting upwards,
long smooth ripples—not gauging how near she was
to the oozing resin of a wound in the tree,

till she blundered two right front feet
into viscous yellow and then
could not resist the momentum of more feet
pressing from behind, tried to push away
from that gummy mess,
her ninety-eight feet thrown in reverse,
but the resin's moving too—the stuff has taken her in.

Panicked, she turned her head three-quarter round
to look at the admirable length of herself still free—
to see if she could bend a dozen knees,
or back the heels of the thirty-third pair,
but drooped, instead a front fang too far.

Exchange of Visits

—for Margaret of Aughton nr Ormskirk

Sultry air and bright summer clouds belie the actual October,
and mosquitoes for now sleep in the shore grass.
A Louisiana Heron casts a crested shadow beside the pier.
Joe Boudreaux bullies us to his boat, a craw-fishing boat,
he says, with Bill, his mannerly, gray-eyed, Catahoula hound.

We're far from tattoos at Edinburgh Castle
and the Black Rocks along the North Sea last year,
where we hiked around one great sharply-pointing finger
to see the Guillemots at their nests.
We were damp in the flying sea mist,
wary of surf-boom below.

Our boat cuts the Atchafalaya Basin's miles of mirror
which melt to brown tea next to the boat,
then shoves at great floating mats of yellow flowering.
Looking back, we see them disturbed
far longer than we hoped by a serpentine, drifting division.
The Basin's silent and still, but for our mechanical
putt-putt and transient wake.
Joe slows through moss-strewn cypress and iron wood,
ancient oaks spread on occasional islets, vast flooded tracts
marked for those who can read
the tell-tales flying on skeletal stakes.
Boudreaux tells about himself:
how his Cajun blood is swamp-water,
how he gave up other trades for this one.

We're far from dry chalk Stonehenge mysteries
and the Great House Charlecote, near Stratford,
where the Lucy Family held for seven hundred years
with their fences and tame herds of red deer.
I have the feather presented by the peacock himself.

At the high point of the swamp tour,
Boudreaux shuts off the motor, and we drift,
while Bill rises, staring off the starboard bow.
Ah, the biggest alligator of them all,
a dragon fit for St. George to try.

GRIEVERS

The dying is what she did—
        The grieving is what we do.
We don't know what she was learning,
        The long lessons through the months.

Sometimes she tried to tell us—
        Then we wondered where all her lifelong piety had gone.
        She was querulous and complaining, even bitter.

Much later she was calm and wise,
        And we could look on and admire her at last
            Because now she didn't ask for much:
                To walk beside her, pour a glass of water,
                Adjust the window blinds.

It was she who gave the benedictions, lying back
        Weary and loving.

We learned nothing of dying and death.
        We've learned little about grief
            We hadn't known already.
        After all, we've grieved our disappointments
            And knives to the heart since infancy.

Even in our ignorance,
        I guess we can say that grieving
            Doesn't cost as much.

We don't know what she found out,
        Nor how to do what she did
            Before our eyes.

Cork Sculpture

In this glass box, blooming shrubs crown
a mossy cliff, *pen jing* style,
two cranes for good fortune;
the first on his islet probes a fan palmetto;
the second cranes sharply round
towards the pagoda in the center.
At the other side a very tall tree
climbs to its own glass sky.

See rows of tile on the roof,
tiny fretwork on the ridges;
the roof arcing down and out in Oriental sweep
to rampant dragons on the corners.
Double rows of columns, outer and inner,
rise to scalloped soffit beams
to support a latticed wall.
A balustrade leads five broad steps
down to black lacquer,
for the building sits on an isthmus,
out to its craggy cork edges, front and rear.

The sculptor carved the pagoda,
box inside a box, around a stillness,
a mystery we cannot see.
Our steadiest gaze passes through
the glass and columns and lattice,
to the flowered wallpaper of our room—
box within a box.

Yet while we look the stillness grows,
and we have it for a moment as our own.

Remembering Houses

Checking behind the panel of the bluebird box,
we glimpsed a stack of nests from prior years
collapsed and pressed by another on top.
Later, I lifted the roof just enough to reach down
in the small dark, till my fingers touched
a silken softness, mere seconds, not wanting to disturb
the fledglings more than I already had,
and, so briefly, their radiant, pliable warmth.

I have my own stacked nests:
the home place where I was born,
the city duplex when I was four,
the new house in the 'burbs,
my ephemeral fourth, fifth, sixth—college days—
pliable to the touch—
later more: rented, shared, borrowed, or bought.

Each home we struggle to furnish
with what we need or desire,
tangible or intangible,
where we can lay our heads through stormy nights
in leaves, straw, twigs, down, spit, bits of cellophane,
a square molded to the box we're in,
till the nest outlives convenience,
so we migrate, hopeful, to build anew.

My latest nest rests on a stack of nests,
my mind reaching down in the small dark
to the former preserved beneath,
prior foundations and bones,
an archaeology of boxes.

Selah Ranch, Texas

The rancher bends down to the limestone
we're all standing on and whisks away
with his brush the chalky detritus
and unnameable tiny accumulations
in the hollows there
and we stare
breathless to see
emerging from his careful ministrations
the huge prints, the pads, the toe-ruts
gouged in Pleistocene alluvium,
the cut of a dew-claw behind,
unmistakable to the last skeptic
among us.
Nearby, more brushing, a second path
angles across the first, having
smudged the former print a little,
letting us know
that where we stand now
was a good, teeming place.
We say Ah! when we recover breath
and point like children
alive to our lost Earth companions
thrilling us with their casual purpose.

THE PELICANS

Lake Darling, Iowa

From the parking lot I suppose a white snow bank,
the last drift of winter—
or white boulders edging the lake.
Nearer, I see the white move,
lift heavy shapes of gold
slow-motion and like rows of dominoes,
one great wave.

I arrive to rows of White Pelicans,
three, four, nine abreast,
shoulders touching, gliding.
Till a perturbation begins,
a tensing to a white blur and ruffle—
a mass commotion of rick-rack
against the trees on the far shore—
and, heads below, they feed!

I hold my breath, and they turn together
on axles, beaks skyward, pouches drooping:
an encore, applause. The vanguard bows
in perfection—the next row and the next row bows,
ablaze on the lake's dark surface.
A single Great Blue Heron on the opposite shore
attends their progress.

Sparrows

A flock follows the most vigilant and wary bird.
At the first twitch of his wing, they rise in a cloud
as we appear on the path in the distance.

They make a smoky tower, then bank in mid-air,
as Blue Angels do after years of practice. Swooping
at pitched angle from where they were scattered

on the ground, they settle on a bush, like ashes.
Some mistake at first wind and twig, as they fall to another twig,
hammer-locked by the wind, but holding on.

We marvel at the uncommon sight, the instant,
concerted physicality. We thank them as if
they had performed for us, and, in a way, they had.

I Become a Tree

The sun's angle at eight in December
        throws a sharp shadow of my cat
low against the fence,
        her straight back, ears.

I thought of rushing out
        with a bucket of black paint
to capture the silhouette,
        but she and the shape soon
merged with the salvia.

Last week's Song Sparrow
        visits me still, but has turned into a Savannah.

I have wondered where the wild birds
        survive a frosty night, and today I found
the tree, the very hole, owned by a Winter Wren.

Now I'm a metamorphosis, a miracle
        to a House Finch banging himself a dozen times
against the back porch ceiling
        till I stretched out my arm
and he settled on my elbow.

I was a tree
        which somehow conveyed him
                toward the yard
                        and the open sky,
where he left me in a flutter.

WEAVINGS

I've gathered this backyard, placed the pieces,
the string hammock angled to the fence
under a scant, feathery desert willow, which—
while I'm stretched out in the twilight,
looking through the leaves at the sky I chose—
rains down pink trumpets like orchids.

In childhood, didn't some trees murmur,
even on windless days?*
In old-growth Polish woods, I saw a family
hunting mushrooms, baskets on forearms.
I saw quiet country men in the Wednesday Market,
hunched behind baskets of mushrooms.
I wove a wreath of osier to hang on my door.

Door wreath, a basket, pageantry of market days,
a hammock angled to the corner,
murmuring trees who are weaving soil and light,
a poem hung finally on its page:
all weavings a prayer for another beauty.

*Sentence quoted from *Another Beauty,* by Adam Zagajewski, Farar, Straus and Giroux, 2000

Mary Ellen Branan was born in rural Caldwell Parish in North Louisiana, raised in Houston, and educated at the University of Texas, Austin, and the University of Houston. She was an "English major," then a social worker, psychotherapist and college teacher for a number of years. Finally, she studied poetry at UH (PhD,1991). She served in the Peace Corps in Poland 1994-96. She has also lived in Fairfield, Iowa, and San Francisco, California. She now lives in Bastrop, Texas. Her work has received awards from the Houston International Festival, Houston Poetry Fest, Iowa Poetry Association, Austin Poetry Association, and the Blue Light Press.

Printed in the United States of America

www.ingramcontent.com/pod-product-compliance
Lightning Source LLC
Chambersburg PA
CBHW032030090426
42741CB00006B/794